Dare to Dally with

SKUNKS
& THEIR RELATIVES

Published by Wildlife Education, Ltd.
12233 Thatcher Court, Poway, California 92064
contact us at: **1-800-477-5034**
e-mail us at: **animals@zoobooks.com**
visit us at: **www.zoobooks.com**

ISBN 1-888153-03-2

Skunks &
Their Relatives

Series Created by
John Bonnett Wexo

Written by
Timothy Levi Biel

Scientific Consultants
Leonard Lee Rue III
Wildlife Author & Photographer

Howard Evans, Ph.D.
Chairman
New York College of Veterinary Medicine
Cornell University

Contents

Skunks and their relatives make up a family of mammals known as the mustelids. Besides skunks, this family includes weasels, ferrets, minks, martens, badgers, wolverines, and otters.

People and other animals go out of their way to avoid skunks and most of the skunk's relatives. That is because these animals have a secret weapon. They produce a sticky, smelly liquid called musk. A single squirt of musk is all it takes to keep most animals from bothering a mustelid.

There are 67 different kinds, or *species*, of mustelids. Members of this diverse family occupy most habitats and can be found in all parts of the world except Antarctica and Australia. They eat a variety of foods: fish, birds, insects, small mammals, fruits, roots, garbage, and honey! Their varied sizes, shapes, preferred diets, and hunting methods are all adaptations that let them live successfully in their different habitats.

The body of a mustelid is built low to the ground. It has short legs and a long, flexible backbone. There are many variations of this basic design, from skinny weasels to stocky wolverines. But all are built for capturing prey and eating meat.

Many of them have incredibly slender bodies, like the mink featured on these pages. Such thin bodies are wonderful for turning and twisting through heavy brush, and even for swimming. But those thin bodies don't hold heat well. This is why minks and other mustelids have some of the warmest, most luxurious fur coats in the entire animal kingdom.

The thick, shiny fur of a mink reflects almost every color imaginable. Oils that make the fur waterproof cause the shine.

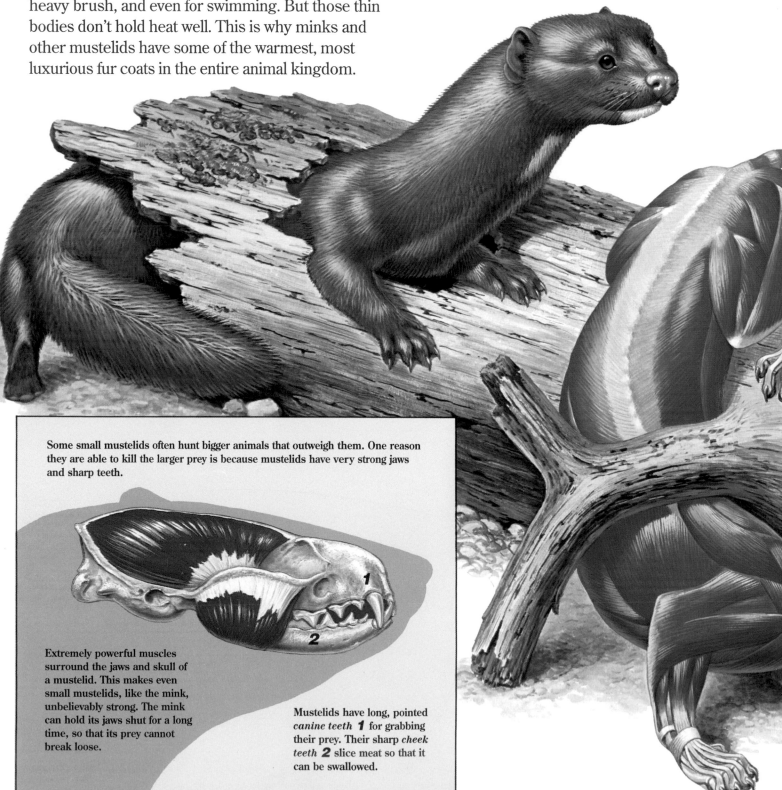

Some small mustelids often hunt bigger animals that outweigh them. One reason they are able to kill the larger prey is because mustelids have very strong jaws and sharp teeth.

Extremely powerful muscles surround the jaws and skull of a mustelid. This makes even small mustelids, like the mink, unbelievably strong. The mink can hold its jaws shut for a long time, so that its prey cannot break loose.

Mustelids have long, pointed *canine teeth* **1** for grabbing their prey. Their sharp *cheek teeth* **2** slice meat so that it can be swallowed.

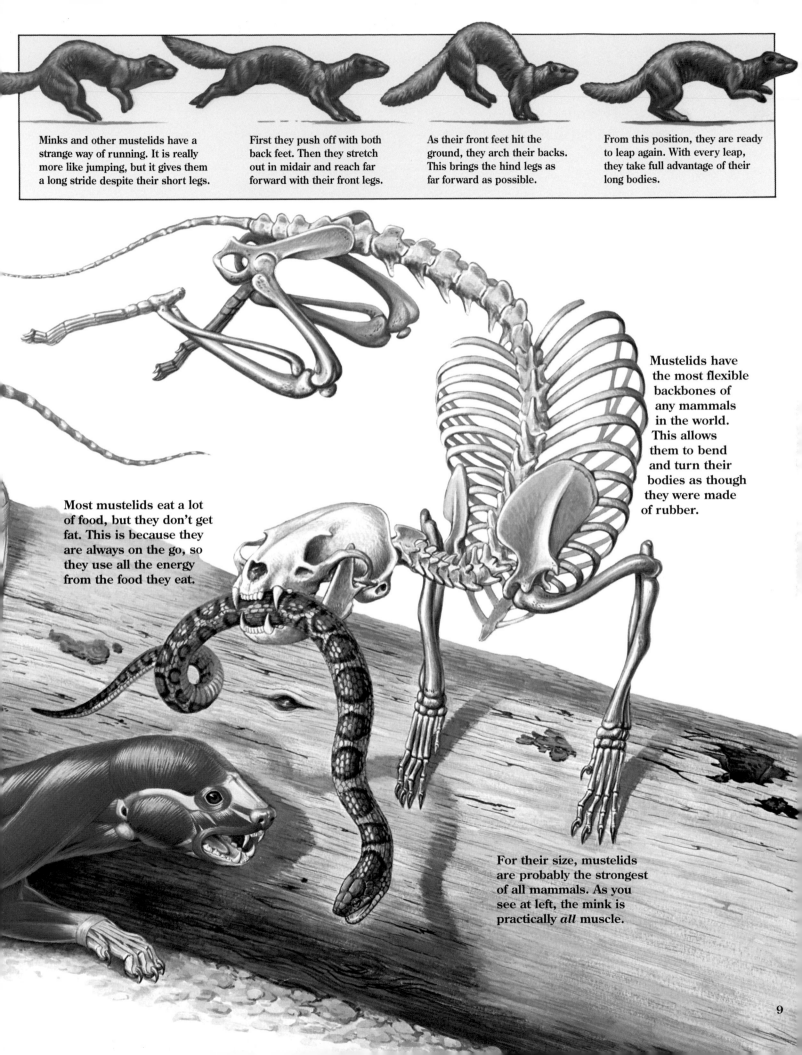

Minks and other mustelids have a strange way of running. It is really more like jumping, but it gives them a long stride despite their short legs.

First they push off with both back feet. Then they stretch out in midair and reach far forward with their front legs.

As their front feet hit the ground, they arch their backs. This brings the hind legs as far forward as possible.

From this position, they are ready to leap again. With every leap, they take full advantage of their long bodies.

Mustelids have the most flexible backbones of any mammals in the world. This allows them to bend and turn their bodies as though they were made of rubber.

Most mustelids eat a lot of food, but they don't get fat. This is because they are always on the go, so they use all the energy from the food they eat.

For their size, mustelids are probably the strongest of all mammals. As you see at left, the mink is practically *all* muscle.

Weasels are even skinnier than minks. Yet they are probably the most effective hunters in the mustelid family. They are also the hungriest. For their size, weasels eat more food than almost any other predator on earth.

If a weasel stops eating for very long, it will die. Like you, weasels get their energy from the food they eat. But they burn it much faster than you do. Because of this, weasels need a constant food supply. It takes a human about two months to eat its weight in food. A weasel has to eat its weight in food every single day!

When weasels aren't busy hunting, they are often trying to avoid bigger predators that may be hunting *them*. Fortunately, weasels can hide by "disappearing" into the background.

The least weasel usually hunts mice, but if it gets hungry enough, it may even attack a cottontail rabbit that is five or six times as big as the weasel.

LONG-TAILED WEASEL (SUMMER)

The color of the weasel's coat helps it hide. Weasels that live in cold climates change their fur color twice a year. For most of the year, the fur on their head and back is brown. This blends with the colors of the forest, and it helps the weasels to hide from both predators and prey.

HOURS OF DAYLIGHT	NIGHTTIME

HOURS OF DAYLIGHT	NIGHTTIME

LONG-TAILED WEASEL (WINTER)

The fur color changes automatically. It is controlled by the amount of daylight per day. In the winter, when there are few hours of daylight, the weasel grows a white coat that blends with the snow. In the spring, as the hours of daylight increase, it grows a new coat of brown fur.

A weasel cannot even sleep through the night without getting hungry. Fortunately, it has an excellent sense of smell, which helps it to find prey in the dark.

LEAST WEASEL

Most weasels eat anything they can find. But one close relative of the weasel, the black-footed ferret, depends almost entirely on one kind of prey. In the wild, it mostly hunts prairie dogs, and it lives in abandoned prairie dog burrows. Prairie dogs often use an unusual method to combat ferrets. Working together, they quickly fill a ferret's burrow with dirt! The black-footed ferret is now considered extinct in the wild, although captive-bred ferrets are being returned to some appropriate habitats.

Weasels are fearless hunters. They sometimes enter the burrows of large, vicious rats and attack them. The short-tailed weasel at left is fighting one of the biggest and most dangerous rats of all—a Norway rat.

SHORT-TAILED WEASEL, OR ERMINE

Weasels hunt many different kinds of prey. But the short-tailed weasel, or ermine, eats mostly rabbits. Like other weasels, the ermine is curious and stands tall to sniff the air and look around for its next meal. There are also predators that eat weasels. When a weasel looks for a meal, it sometimes becomes a meal! Owls are probably the weasel's greatest enemies. At night, these hunters can silently swoop down and grab a weasel before it has a chance to run away.

11

Skunks are no bigger than housecats. Yet mountain lions, wolves, and even bears run away when they see a skunk, because they don't want to get sprayed. To avoid being sprayed by a skunk, they have to stay a safe distance away. Skunks can spray their musk accurately at objects 15 feet away!

Many people think that skunks spray everything in sight. Actually, they do not like to spray their musk. They use it only when necessary. Most often, these furry little black and white creatures are fun to watch—especially a family of skunks out for an evening walk.

Musk is a skunk's only defense. Because it doesn't have an endless supply of musk, the skunk sprays only if it has to.

Before it sprays, a skunk has several ways to warn an intruder. First, it stomps with its front feet and rakes the ground with its claws.

A mother skunk is a wonderful teacher. She teaches her young how to hunt and dig for food and how to defend themselves. Until they are about six months old, young skunks follow their mother in single file wherever she goes.

Baby skunks are born with their black and white hair. They can spray their musk even before they learn to walk.

STRIPED SKUNK

If the first warning doesn't work, the skunk arches its back, hisses, and raises its tail. In this position, a black and white skunk is easy to see. Its raised tail is like a sign that means, "Stop! Think where you're going!"

For most skunks, the raised tail is its final warning. But a spotted skunk many give one more warning, as shown at right.

Before it sprays, a spotted skunk may do a "handstand." If you see one do this, don't wait around until it gets all its feet on the ground. It can spray while its back legs are in the air!

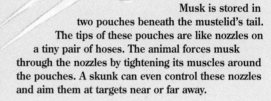

Musk is stored in two pouches beneath the mustelid's tail. The tips of these pouches are like nozzles on a tiny pair of hoses. The animal forces musk through the nozzles by tightening its muscles around the pouches. A skunk can even control these nozzles and aim them at targets near or far away.

Skunks usually don't move very fast. But when they need to be, they are quick enough to catch snakes. This hooded skunk has cornered a gopher snake. Sometimes this species even kills rattlesnakes!

HOODED SKUNK

People have tried almost everything to get the skunk smell out of clothes, hair, and skin. Household bleach is the best thing to use on clothes. But no one has found a secret formula for things that can't be bleached, like hair or skin. Washing them with vinegar or tomato juice probably works the best.

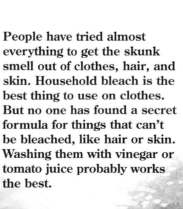

These young river otters are only 12 weeks old.

Badgers are born to dig. They live in deep underground tunnels, and they hunt by breaking into the underground tunnels where other animals live.

When badgers are threatened by predators, they can quickly escape by digging a hole, climbing inside, and filling it up with dirt. Their short powerful legs and long sharp claws can rip through almost anything. People have even seen them working their way through blacktop pavement!

Badgers live in many different parts of the world, and they dig for different kinds of food. The African honey badger, or ratel, digs honeycombs out of tree hollows and rock crevices. To help it find the honeycombs, it often has special helpers.

EUROPEAN BADGER

LONG-TAILED WEASEL

All mustelids have long bodies and short legs. But some are thin and others are not. As you know, weasels have the skinniest bodies. At the other extreme, badgers have the broadest and flattest bodies of all the mustelids.

African honey badgers and little birds called honey guides offer a remarkable example of cooperation. When honey guides see a beehive, they fly off to "tell" a honey badger. The birds circle around the badger and chatter noisily until it follows them to the hive. The badger digs into the hive with its sharp claws and eats the honey. As a reward, the little birds get to eat what is left of the comb.

The badger's flat body is perfect for its way of life. Its body is so wide that a badger can use it to block the entrance to its den. Once it is set in this position, it can fight off almost any attacker. The badger even has folds of loose floppy skin on the sides of its body that make it hard for predators to hunt it. If a predator bites the badger, it may get only a mouthful of loose skin.

AMERICAN BADGER

A badger digs faster with its paws than you can dig with a shovel. That's because each paw has five sturdy claws that are shaped like shovels. A badger digs with 20 shovels at once!

A mother badger takes good care of her young. She keeps the babies inside her den until they are about six weeks old. Then she may let the little badgers go outside to play. When the mother senses danger, she quickly pulls them back inside.

Badgers chase mice, gophers, and even rabbits into their burrows. But when a badger does this, it may accidentally help a coyote get a meal.

A rabbit's burrow usually has two entrances. So when a rabbit hears a badger breaking in, it goes out the other way.

Once in a while, a coyote will follow a badger as it hunts. Just when a rabbit seems to have escaped from the badger, the coyote may be waiting for it.

Wolverines are the strongest mustelids. Some people even call them *skunk bears* because "they smell like skunks and are as strong as bears!" This is an exaggeration, of course, but wolverines look so mean and are so clever that trappers and outdoorsmen have nicknamed them "mountain devils."

The combination of strength, smell, and cunning has made wolverines very unpopular with some people. They cause a lot of mischief by stealing food from people and destroying their property. As you will see, there is a good reason why wolverines do these things. They are simply looking for food. They live in the far north, where food is scarce, so they take food wherever they can find it.

WOLVERINE

A wolverine will eat anything that crosses its path. It may hunt animals that are much larger than it is, or it may steal food from fierce predators.

To catch larger animals, wolverines climb trees. When an animal passes underneath, the wolverine pounces on it and knocks it off its feet. Wolverines even hunt moose and caribou in this way!

The ferocious nature and strong smell of a wolverine are enough to make most large predators abandon their prey. Mountain lions, wolves, and even bears may leave their prey behind when a wolverine approaches.

A wolverine is too small to eat a large animal in one meal, so it saves the leftover meat. To make sure another animal doesn't steal it, the wolverine sprays the meat with musk, then digs a hole and buries it.

A wolverine can eat almost anything, but there are a few exceptions. If it catches a porcupine and tries to eat it, the wolverine may swallow hundreds of porcupine quills. This could kill the wolverine.

Wolverines can make life miserable for trappers. The animals are clever enough to spring traps without getting caught in them.

A trapper returning to his cabin may find that a wolverine has broken in, ripped everything to shreds, and sprayed its horrible-smelling musk on anything it could not eat.

Trappers often hang food or bait in trees to keep animals from getting it. This doesn't stop the wolverine!

Wolverines are superb trackers that follow their prey almost anywhere. They climb trees, cross rivers, and go over mountains. They even follow their prey into dark places, like caves and hollow logs. They will follow an animal for days, if necessary.

WOLVERINE

Wolverines are aggressive hunters, but they have never been known to attack people. Yet even the bravest person doesn't want to get too close to a wolverine. Its musk reeks like the musk of a skunk. If the smell gets on clothes or skin, it lingers for days.

19

Otters spend most of their time in the water. Their long, thin bodies are ideal for swimming. Powerful tails push them along, and webs on their hands and feet help them steer. Their thick fur coats keep them warm in cold water. The sea otter has the thickest fur of any animal on earth.

Most otters live in freshwater rivers, but there are some that live in the ocean too. Wherever they live, all otters love to play. They pass many hours frolicking and exploring their surroundings. This curiosity and love of games has made otters the most popular with people of all the mustelids.

River otters need long stretches of clean, open water. Unfortunately, as time goes by, more and more rivers become polluted. This means there are fewer places for otters to live.

River otters never seem to get enough mud sliding! They slide down steep riverbanks and dive headfirst into the water. Then they climb back up the riverbank and wait their turn to slide down again. They may keep this up for hours!

Otters often use their webbed feet like rudders to steer them as they swim.

Sea otters dive for abalone, sea urchins, and other shellfish. They usually find them at the bottom of the sea where there are large beds of seaweed.

After the otter finds a shellfish, it picks up a large, flat rock. It tucks the rock in a flap of skin under its arm, holds the shellfish in its front paws, and carries the rock and the shellfish back to the surface.

River otters move almost as well on land as they do in the water. Their long toes give them a good grip on the ground, so they can run quickly.

SEA OTTER

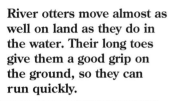

RIVER OTTER

Once it reaches the surface, the sea otter floats on its back and puts the rock on its chest. Holding the shellfish in both hands, it pounds it against the rock until the shell cracks.

Sea otters spend almost all of their time in the water. Their front paws have short, stubby fingers that make it awkward for them to move on land. But short fingers are perfect for swimming and scooping up shellfish.

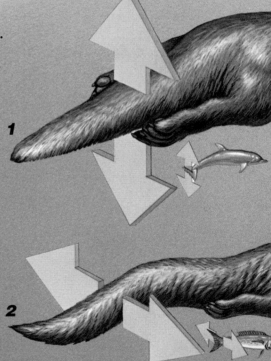

1

2

A river otter has to be a fast swimmer in order to catch a fish. Its favorite method for catching one is to chase the fish into a shallow inlet where it can be cornered.

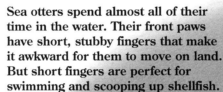

When the otter is sure the fish cannot escape, it catches it in its mouth. Then it carries the fish up onto the bank and eats it.

Sea otters swim in deeper water than river otters do, so they use their tails differently. The sea otter's tail **1** is broader and flatter than the river otter's **2**. When it swims, the sea otter moves its tail up and down as a dolphin does. The river otter moves its tail as a fish does—from side to side.

21

The future can be hopeful for most mustelids. In North America, South America, India, and Asia, about a dozen species are considered endangered or vulnerable to extinction. The main reasons for the decline in numbers are habitat loss and destruction, and hunting and trapping.

Much of North America was first explored by trappers looking for fur, and they gathered millions of mustelid furs. Before fur trapping was controlled, minks, martens, and otters were nearly driven to extinction.

The black-footed ferret, thought to be North America's rarest animal, is an example of what happens when nature's balance is disturbed. Until the mid-1980s, a few black-footed ferrets still lived on the western prairies. The ferret depended on the prairie dog for about 90 percent of its food. Underground prairie dog "towns" once riddled the Great Plains, fed ferrets, and annoyed farmers and ranchers. In an effort to protect wheat farmers' crops and to save the prairie grasses for grazing cattle and sheep, government-sponsored programs began to eradicate the prairie dog. In Kansas alone, more than 98 percent of the prairie dog colonies were destroyed.

With the prairie dog population decimated, the ferret had little to eat and died out. In 1985, the last remaining ferrets in the wild were captured for captive breeding, with the hope to eventually return the species to the wild. The U. S. Fish and Wildlife Service reports that there are 10 places in North America with prairie dog colonies large enough to support ferrets. Some captive-born ferrets have been released, but there is no wild population yet. It is hoped that by 2010 there will be 1,500 ferrets divided into 10 or more populations. That could improve the ferret's status from endangered to threatened. For now, the ferret is considered extinct in the wild.

Ecological destruction affects a variety of mustelids. People pollute rivers where minks and otters hunt. They cut trees for timber where martens make their homes. And rodent control accidentally poisons other mustelids. As a group, mustelids kill more rodents than any other group of predators. We should help them rather than harm them.

Martens look like weasels with long, bushy tails. But instead of running along the ground looking for mice, they dart over tree branches and hunt squirrels. The marten's long, bushy tail helps it balance as it scampers through the treetops. This is a beech marten, which occupies woodlands from Europe to central Asia.

Index